YOUR COMPLETE
GUIDE TO

First published in Great Britain in 2008 by
GA Publishing, part of Civil Ceremonies Ltd

1 3 5 7 9 10 8 6 4 2

Any correspondence regarding this publication should be addressed to:
The Managing Director, Civil Ceremonies Ltd, PO Box 160, St Neots, Cambs PE19 5WL

A CIP catalogue record for this book is available
from the British Library.

ISBN-13: 978-0-9560228-0-6

Designed by Gemma Barber
Printed in Great Britain by Cambrian Printers using papers from FSC sources.

GA
PUBLISHING

YOUR COMPLETE GUIDE TO

Naming
CEREMONIES

written by
ANNE BARBER

with foreword by
BEL MOONEY

This book is dedicated to Michael Young, Lord Young of Dartington, who had the vision to know that these ceremonies would be important to families.

Born on August 9th 1915, Young became a towering figure in post-Second World War social policymaking, but is perhaps most famous for inventing the Open University and the Consumers' Association.

Michael Young was a man of phenomenal energy whose vital contributions to British 20th century social reform earned him a life peerage in 1978.

Lord Young established the Baby Naming Society in 1994 and was instrumental to the introduction of baby naming ceremonies in 1998 by the then Home Secretary, Jack Straw. The concept was seen as a secular answer to the decline in Church of England baptisms, and was a key part of the Government's plan to reverse the decline of family life in Britain.

Lord Young was a pioneer of social ideas and institutions who remained an active social innovator until his death on January 14th 2002, at the age of 86.

Remembered with great affection.

No matter how sophisticated we become, great moments in life still fill us with awe. Birth, marriage, death….these are the most significant punctuation marks in an individual's lifetime, giving meaning. We could add coming-of-age, betrothal, big birthdays, retirement….moments marked by the pop of a cork, affectionate speeches, gifts. Such events speak of the eternal human need for ritual. They link us with our first ancestors who raised arms in unison to the sky.

The need for ritual does not diminish in a sceptical age. Some who never set foot in church seek to 'use' it for marriages and christenings. They may have good reason. But how much more honest to mark the solemn joy of the momentous event with a civil ceremony, or a ritual of your own devising. I've been to a self-organised, secular wedding and a funeral and both were truly wonderful – because of the creative love that had devised them. But easier for some people is to use the skills of a trained celebrant who has the right words to guide them through.

About one third of UK families fail to celebrate their new babies in any formal way. In my opinion, they are missing out. You may not want a traditional christening, yet the alternative – a Naming Ceremony – acknowledges the importance of the new arrival in front of family and friends who *witness*. This book will guide all parents (and step-parents, and others) in search of suitable words and rituals to welcome their new baby into our human family.

Bel mooney

Journalist and Writer

Not so very long ago it was the norm in the UK to have a child baptised. It was almost a given. So why are so many thousands of people – people just like you – now choosing instead to welcome their child into the world with a Naming Ceremony?

Well, you need only look at the amount of social change in the last few decades to see why. Probably the most significant change is the steady increase in Civil Marriages. In 2006, according to the Office of National Statistics, 66% of marriages were Civil. In other words, religious marriages are now a minority.

In fact, since the Second World War – a time responsible for many significant social changes – church attendance itself has steadily declined. Many people who marry in church are not churchgoers,

and people more commonly marry more than once in their lifetime. All of this has contributed to a marked decline in the number of baptisms. In fact, the Church of England now performs baptisms for around just 15% of children.

Couples who don't get married in church invariably find it hypocritical to take their child along for a christening, or baptism. Many couples who do marry in church do so for their own reasons, yet find the religious aspect of a christening inappropriate. There are more stepfamilies these days, too, who want a ceremony which suits their family circumstances. And there are increasing numbers of single parents and cohabiting couple families in the UK. Cohabiting couples increased by 65 percent between 1996 and 2006, from 1.4 million to 2.3 million. So we see

that many people simply don't include the church, or the associated traditional ceremonies, in their lives. What all of this means is that in deciding to have a Naming Ceremony rather than a baptism you are not alone. Far from it.

But with all these social changes and complications, why bother at all? Well many families don't – we estimate that about one third of families in the UK don't undertake any formal welcoming for their child. In many cases it's a conscious decision not to. However, we've found that the most common

sentiment from those who haven't reflects a general regret that they never got round to it or didn't bother.

Commemorating the birth of a child remains, for many families, an important occasion. They, like you, want to mark that wondrous event in a very personal and special way. Many desire a ceremony which is dignified yet relaxed; something meaningful and relevant to their personal values, but which is in no way trivial. An occasion, rather, to make very public and personal declarations of love and support, and to celebrate

the joy of parenthood with family and friends.

When Naming Ceremonies were first made available in the UK they were seen by some as alternative; perhaps in the same way that Civil Marriages were seen at their inception. In today's society, a Naming Ceremony is a positive decision in its own right – a desire simply to have a meaningful ceremony to celebrate the birth of a child.

What could be more natural or more wonderful?

This book will guide you through the creation and development of your own unique and very personal day. It's packed full of information to help you make the right choices for you, and to help you organise everything; whether you choose to have the ceremony conducted by someone you know, or by a professional Celebrant.

Arranging something like this can be, for some, a daunting endeavour. In fact, it's really quite straightforward. You'll certainly have a whole host of questions – rest assured this book will answer all of them. We cover every aspect of the ceremony itself, the decisions you need to make, how to arrange it all and how to make it the perfect centrepiece of a wonderful family event. Above all we'll help you relax so that you can just enjoy what will undoubtedly be one of the most joyous occasions of your life.

> "Looking back now, we feel that a Naming Ceremony has been even more personal than a traditional Christening as all aspects of it were chosen by us. I would highly recommend a Naming Ceremony to anyone who wants to mark their child's arrival into this world but doesn't feel a religious ceremony is appropriate. Just such a beautiful day for everyone – hardly a dry eye in the house – lovely."

About naming ceremonies

So what exactly is a Naming Ceremony?

One answer that springs to mind is "It's exactly what you want it to be!" Actually, that sums up quite nicely the fact that a Naming Ceremony is unique. Yours will be planned by you, with the help of this book, and because it'll include your own very personal choices it will most definitely be one of a kind.

But perhaps we need to take a step back before we go any further and explore precisely what a Naming Ceremony is, what it isn't and why people have them.

What a Naming Ceremony is

Having a baby is, without doubt, one of the most wonderful events in anyone's life. So it stands to reason that you want to celebrate it. A Naming Ceremony is a very special way of doing that. It's a highly personal and meaningful event that's designed to actively welcome your child into the family.

Moreover, it's something that you construct to reflect your own personal values. It's an opportunity to declare, in front of your family and friends, your promise to be the very best parent you can be. And it's in words of your choosing; derived from your values – not those of a stranger's doctrine.

But it's also much more than that. It's about focusing attention on your child's future development and the valuable contribution that will be made by your wider family and your closest friends. It's a time for all the people who will play an integral role in your child's upbringing – his or her Supporting Adults – to also make declarations of love and ongoing encouragement and protection.

In short, it's about binding everyone together in a tangible circle of support that's focused on your child's future.

What it isn't

A Naming Ceremony is something you choose to do. There are no legal requirements, stipulations or consequences for you or anyone else who's involved, nor is anyone legally bound by the promises they make. A Naming Ceremony is a personal choice – not a legal one.

• It doesn't replace or complement your legal requirement to register the birth of a child with your local Register Office.

• Any certificate of the event is purely for your own use, to enhance the event and provide a lasting reminder of the promises you and the child's Supporting Adults have made. It can't be used for identification purposes or to change a child's name.

Just so you know. . .

Some Local Authorities offer Naming Ceremonies, many of which are supplied by Civil Ceremonies Ltd. A Register Office may ask to see your child's birth certificate merely as a precaution to ensure you have legal jurisdiction over the child and to prove you've registered the birth. Naming Ceremonies organised by other providers, including Civil Ceremonies Ltd, don't require this.

So, why have a Naming Ceremony?

There are many reasons why people choose to have one. In many ways it's the flexibility of a Naming Ceremony that makes it such an appropriate choice. Your reasons will be unique to you, but these are some of the most common reasons people have given us:

"We want to welcome our child in a unique way into our family and circle of friends.

We don't have any particular faith and so don't wish to have a religious ceremony.

We don't have the same faith and don't want to commit our child to one or the other.

We want to celebrate a new member of the family and acknowledge our daughter's identity by formally announcing her name.

We want to promise our child that we will be the best parents we can be.

We don't go to church and we don't therefore want to make specific promises that aren't relevant and which we don't really intend to keep.

We want a party to celebrate the birth of our son but want to give it a proper focus."

What about adopted children or step-children?

What better way to 'officially' welcome adopted children or step-children into their new family than with a Naming Ceremony?

Families who take the very special step of adopting a child find that a Naming Ceremony is a particularly valuable and important way of binding the new family unit. It's a wonderful way of welcoming the child to their circle of family and friends and helps create a real sense of 'belonging'. One of the great things about a Naming Ceremony is that it's suitable for children of any age – not just babies.

Although the 'naming' part is significant, the most important aspect of the ceremony is that you're communicating

In our 2007 customer survey the top reasons for having arranged a Naming Ceremony were:

Appointing Supporting Adults	24%
Welcoming the baby	23%
Getting friends and family together	23%
Making special parents' promises	19.5%
A party to celebrate the baby	10%
Involving grandparents	0.5%

your commitment to the child, to their welfare and to their future happiness. The same thing applies when a new baby is born into a family that already includes children from a previous marriage. Older children can sometimes feel like they're no longer the centre of attention, so involving them in a Naming Ceremony is the perfect way to show them they're special too.

Multi-faith ceremonies

A Naming Ceremony is the perfect solution where parents belong to different faiths. The ceremony can have no religious or cultural content at all, or could include something of both faiths to truly represent the combined values of both parents.

What families say...
"This was a lovely way to welcome our daughter into the world."
"This was so important to us – it was the best day ever."

And another thing...

Any parent can arrange a Naming Ceremony; it doesn't matter whether you're married to the child's other parent, you are a single parent or whether you have any religious or spiritual beliefs. In fact, many parents who are not married feel a Naming Ceremony has added significance, since it may be the first real opportunity to get both sides of the family together for a special event.

Your child,
your ceremony

What kind of ceremony do you want?

As with a Christening, a Naming Ceremony doesn't have any legal status but it is, nevertheless, a sincere and meaningful occasion. But it's also a celebration. Getting the balance right is important, and exactly where the balance should be needs careful thought.

You've probably got more than one reason for deciding to have a Naming Ceremony, but what is your primary reason? When you pinpoint that you'll have a pretty good idea of the tone you'll want to adopt for the ceremony. That will help you choose the most appropriate wording and ensure it really does reflect how you feel.

Don't forget, the ceremony itself is part of a much wider family event. It's the centrepiece of that event, certainly, and you'll want it to be special and exactly right. There are innumerable ways to enhance and augment it to create an event that everyone will talk about for years to come. More about that later.

Remember, it's your ceremony. . .

Naming Ceremonies are becoming more and more popular and it's the natural choice for many families. Some people - perhaps of an older generation, or because of their religious beliefs - may not agree with your choice. However, they do need to respect your wishes and appreciate how important the ceremony is to you.

Where will its focus be?

A religious ceremony for any faith has, at its core, the relationship between the child and the church or the God of that religion. A Naming Ceremony on the other hand is about the core relationship between the parents and their child. In choosing to have a Naming Ceremony what you're saying, in effect, is that you want the focus of the ceremony to be your love for your child. Everything else is secondary.

An important conversation

Parents discuss every aspect of their new baby at great length, from the colour of the nursery to their choice of school later on, but how often is there a real discussion on what type of parents you want to be?

Planning your child's Naming Ceremony is an ideal time to have that conversation, because as part of the ceremony you'll make sincere and personal promises and it's obviously important you agree on them. It's often assumed that you think the same but sometimes differences do emerge; not necessarily about the fundamental principles of parenthood, but perhaps about the ideals and values you most want to instill.

Just so you know . . .
Having a Naming Ceremony has no effect whatsoever on the child's future decisions to either be baptised or marry in church.

And another thing. . .
There's no reason why you shouldn't have both a religious ceremony and a Naming Ceremony if you want to – some families do and tell us this worked well for them. For other parents, there are religious or spiritual readings or poems that have special meaning for them. There's no reason why you shouldn't include them if that's what you want. It's your ceremony!

What are the most important things you want to promise your child?

What are the values and ethics you want your child to embrace as he or she grows up? Will you teach tolerance and respect for the rights of others? Are you determined that your child will develop a strong sense of right and wrong? Do you want your child to grow up with a strong sense of responsibility for protecting the planet?

The promises that you make to your child during the ceremony can be as simple as saying that you will be as good a parent as you can, to a long list of everything that you wish for your child now and in the future.

By thinking about the special promises you want to publicly make to your child, you're effectively clarifying and defining your values. They're the values that you'll naturally want your child to embrace as he or she grows up.

Your child's name

The actual naming of your child is an important part of the ceremony because it establishes identity and individuality. You also have an opportunity to share your reasons for your choice of name. That choice could have a real significance that you want to share with everyone.

Top Tip!

If you haven't made a Will now is the time to do so. The absence of a Will would have serious consequences for your child if you die. More information about Wills is available from: www.adviceguide.org.uk

Your thoughts, your way

Parenthood is a time of profound change, and for some parents the Naming Ceremony is an appropriate occasion to acknowledge this by also making vows and promises to each other. This could involve re-stating your marriage vows or simply making a declaration of commitment and support to each other.

There's also an opportunity to express your innermost thoughts and feelings on parenthood and your memories and hopes for the future. Your words will be personal to you, but here's how other parents have put it…

Mother

"Motherhood will bring its share of tears and heartaches, but it will teach me hope and patience. It will show me the depth, strength and power of love. It won't always be easy and I'm sure I shall make mistakes, but my baby will grow up all too quickly, so these childhood days are to savour as precious moments to relive again and again.

Father

Being a father is offering me so many new things. I would recognise my baby's cry if she were in a football stadium of crying children. When she laughs, I have to laugh too. Helen is a guest in our home, to be loved and nurtured but never owned. It will be in helping Helen's dreams to come true that my own dreams will be fulfilled."

What about godparents?

Our friends are very important at the new-baby stage of life; often as important as family members who might live great distances away. It's the people we've gone through pregnancy with; those we call our closest friends, who we especially want to take part in a Naming Ceremony along with our family members. Within this broader group of people are those you'd naturally select to be godparents.

Some parents feel awkward about using the term godparents in a non-religious context. However, a glance in a modern dictionary will tell you it's someone who acts as a godparent, or is a sponsor or protector. A popular alternative is Supporting Adults, but you could equally call them Sponsors.

Whatever you decide to call them, their appointment is obviously extremely important. Although they'll not be legally bound or obliged in any way, they will have a moral obligation to exemplify the promises of support you'll be asking them to make, and they should be prepared to live up to them. By definition they'll be people who have a special relationship with both you and your child. They'll be people who can provide a positive influence and stability as he or she grows up. And you can choose as many as you like, avoiding the common conundrum of trying to choose between two or three particularly suitable couples.

We'll discuss the role Supporting Adults play in more depth in the chapter entitled 'Key roles'.

Top Tip! Avoid using the term 'guardian' (unless legally appropriate) – it may cause confusion because it has a very definite legal connotation.

And grandparents?

One of the great things about a Naming Ceremony is the flexibility it gives you to involve all the people who are important in your child's life. Giving recognition to grandparents and acknowledging the role they will play in your child's life could be a very important part of your ceremony.

In our day-to-day 21st century lives we're used to having more influence than ever before over the things we do and the way we do them. We expect greater choice, too. Naming Ceremonies reflect this and are as personal as you want to make them. They can include anything you feel appropriate to suit your own personal circumstances and requirements. The most important thing is to work out the type of ceremony that you really do want for your child, what you want to say and who you want to be there. If you stick to the things that matter most to you and include them in the event, you will have a wonderful day and the memories of it will last a lifetime.

The venue

Naming Ceremonies can be large and elaborate events, not dissimilar to a wedding reception, or they can involve just you, your child and a few close family and friends. They can be held pretty much anywhere, from a lavish hotel to your own back garden, and cost anything from a few hundred pounds to a few thousand. The choice is yours. However, the number of guests you want to invite will influence where you have the ceremony.

Reflections of a wedding?

Many couples choose to hold the Naming Ceremony at the venue where they held their civil marriage ceremony or wedding reception. Indeed, what could be more romantic?

If it's an expensive venue and you're having fewer guests this time, it's worth considering a smaller room. If it's neither convenient nor appropriate to use the same venue, you can still reflect the theme of the wedding itself elsewhere. You can do this by co-ordinating colours, using the top of the cake (if you still have it) as the Naming Cake, and by asking those who played a role in the wedding to also be involved in the Naming Ceremony. Guests you choose to deliver a reading or introduce a toast could enhance the continuity by referring back to the wedding. Another idea is to hold the Naming Ceremony on your anniversary and use the occasion to display your wedding photographs.

Just so you know . . .
A Naming Ceremony is a private function - the venue doesn't have to be licensed in any way to hold one.

A hotel ceremony

A hotel is naturally a popular ceremony venue. For wedding ceremonies, the venue has to be licensed and staff will be familiar with co-operating fully with the bride and groom's every need. Since the venue doesn't need to be licensed in any way to hold a Naming Ceremony, the hotel you choose may not be used to holding events of this nature. There are, then, a number of things you'll want to consider:

- Is the hotel familiar with the requirements of a ceremony? For example, you'll want guaranteed peace and quiet while the ceremony itself is in progress.

- Is there sufficient parking?

- Is the room easily accessible for all your guests?

- Is the room big enough for all your guests and will the hotel lay it out for you beforehand to your instructions, and provide a table for the Celebrant to use?

- If you want the hotel to provide drinks for a toast, will they co-operate by bringing it in at the right time, and not pop corks just at the wrong moment?!

- If you're providing a cake will they plate it for you?

At a restaurant

Maybe you have a favourite restaurant you can take over for the whole event? This exclusivity provides the event with a very special intimacy, and gives you a great deal of control and privacy. What's more, a friendly host should give you the freedom to configure and decorate the venue however you wish.

Local community venues

Village halls, cricket pavilions and community halls all make ideal venues if you prefer a less formal setting. They'll also give you the flexibility to provide your own catering, which could help you with budgeting for the event.

Just so you know . . .

If you're having a professional Celebrant, he or she will make an appointment to meet you at the venue (whether a hotel, your home or elsewhere) to discuss the ceremony and familiarise themselves with the venue. If you choose a venue that isn't relatively local to you, the ceremony provider will allocate a Celebrant from that locality.

A taste for the unusual

Many ceremonies have been combined with a great day out and if you have a local tourist attraction, such as a zoo or children's farm, they probably have a room to hire out for just this sort of event. Theme parks, too, have function rooms available, and after the ceremony everyone can enjoy the rest of the day making the most of the facilities. This can also take the pressure off you to provide lavish refreshments.

Or how about a castle or stately home? If this appeals to you check with your local tourist information centre for a list of appropriate venues.

Ceremonies at home

If you want to hold the ceremony at home consider first whether the house is really big enough. Do you have a room that will comfortably hold all the people you want to invite? If lots of children and babies will be coming make allowances for their buggies, baby seats and baby equipment as well.

There's also the question of refreshments and any entertainment you might want to provide after the ceremony. If you book a professional Celebrant to lead the ceremony, that person will want to visit the home to check that it's suitable – that doesn't mean it has to be posh or grand, but it does have to be able to cope with the movement of people necessary in a ceremony.

A ceremony at home is definitely the cheapest option – you save not only on room hire but also on catering, and many parents find it less stressful than opting for a hired venue.

Top Tip!
Ceremonies in very public places, like a park or a beach, aren't recommended because they're very difficult to control. It's all too easy for a ceremony to be ruined by noise, wandering dogs or troublesome folk.

Timing can be more flexible and your child isn't daunted by unfamiliar surroundings. On the other hand it can be hard work so you'll probably want to arrange for some friends to help out on the day. Of course, it doesn't have to be your home. If a friend or relative has a more suitable home how about asking if they'd be prepared to host your ceremony?

How to work out if a home ceremony is feasible . . .

- The starting point is to work out how many guests you want to invite.

- Do you have an indoor room (or space for a marquee) big enough to hold everyone? You'll need a table for the Celebrant to use, and there should be available seating for the main participants at least. In fact, it's preferable that everyone, especially older guests and those with children, can sit down if they want to.

- Can friends and family help with food and drink?

In the garden

With a large garden an outdoor ceremony can be lovely, especially if it's followed by a barbecue or picnic buffet. If you wish, it's easy to spread the cost by asking guests to contribute to the refreshments. A garden ceremony also offers all sorts of possibilities for enhancing the event, maybe by releasing balloons or planting a tree in honour of the child. Unfortunately the weather can't be relied upon even at the height of summer, so there always has to be an inside room where the ceremony can be held if the weather does its worst.

Top Tip!
There's not much you can do about passing aeroplanes, but you'll not want your ceremony disturbed by lawnmowers or a bonfire. It's worth making neighbours aware of your plans, or even inviting them to the event.

A marquee

Marquees are terrific as they keep both wet weather and blazing sun at bay. It gives the impression of being outside and offers the appeal of a garden party that will go on well after the ceremony.

It doesn't have to be huge – a local marquee hire company will have a variety of options, and you can even buy a marquee very inexpensively these days from some of the larger DIY stores.

A Welcoming Lunch

If you want a low-key event with just a few close friends and family a welcoming lunch might be an appropriate option. It involves little more than a series of short speeches from key people that they write themselves. This is a much more informal and unstructured event that has much less scope than a Naming Ceremony, but may suit your circumstances and requirements.

A simple event like this could, for example, be opened by dad welcoming everyone and explaining how his life has been altered by the arrival of their baby. After the first course mum could make a speech including why the name has been chosen, and explains who the

The venue

Top Tip!
Be aware of potential hazards from marquee ropes and trailing wires. If you have a pond consider roping it off so other parents of young children don't worry about it.

Supporting Adults will be. After the next course one of the Supporting Adults, on behalf of them all, says how delighted they are to have a special relationship with the baby and how they hope to contribute towards the child's upbringing. At the end of the meal dad asks the guests to raise their glasses for a toast to the baby's future.

When to hold your ceremony

There are a number of considerations when deciding the best time for your Naming Ceremony. Like weddings, the summer months are much more popular for ceremonies than the winter months. However, the time of year your child was born may well influence when you have yours, especially if you want to have the ceremony at a specific stage in your child's life. This can, of course, have a knock-on effect on your chosen venue, particularly if you want to have the ceremony outdoors.

Your child's age

It's probably ideal to wait until your baby is at least a few months old. Most parents are too exhausted by the extra work and sleepless nights to consider it before then! In reality, though, when you do hold the ceremony is entirely up to you and it can take place at any time, even when the child is several years' old.

Just so you know . . .
Civil Ceremonies Ltd provides special ceremonies all year round – and extra special ceremonies for birthdays and Christmas time.

A special date

All your child's early birthdays are significant, but a first birthday is extra special. Not surprisingly this is a very popular time to hold a Naming Ceremony. Other popular times of year include your wedding anniversary, Easter, Christmas or to coincide with a date when family who live overseas are visiting.

If you want to book a professional Celebrant for a bank holiday weekend, we suggest booking early as these are extremely popular dates.

Time and day

Most ceremonies naturally take place at weekends, although you can book a professional Celebrant for any day of the week. What time the actual ceremony starts depends on what other plans you have for the day. It usually takes place somewhere between 11.00 am and 6pm. If you can, try to arrange it around your child's normal feeding routine so he or she isn't craving food as the ceremony starts!

How far in advance?

As with any major event it pays to plan ahead as far as you can. Arranging a Naming Ceremony isn't something many people would expect to do at the drop of a hat, and you'll need to give reasonable notice to your guests to ensure they keep the date free. Ceremonies can be arranged at short notice but realistically you ought to plan at least 6 weeks ahead.

Inviting family and friends

While you're in the process of drawing up your guest list you'll probably know who the key players in your ceremony are. It's worthwhile making sure they're available on the date you have in mind before confirming the venue and sending out invitations. The less notice you give, there is more risk that you may be organising the event around these key players. You really want all the Supporting Adults to be there if at all possible and your closest family might be devastated if you book a day when they can't come. When compiling the list don't forget your child's own friends if he or she is old enough to have them.

Just so you know . . .

A range of high quality invitation cards and gift ideas are available from www.civilceremonies.co.uk

A formal invitation

Many people have never been to a Naming Ceremony and won't know what to expect. Sending written invitations gives you the opportunity to overcome any uncertainty, sets the right tone for the event and ensures nobody gets the details wrong.

Naming Ceremony
We would like to invite you to the naming of
On...
At.......................................
From........................... Time...............
We hope you can be with us on this happy occasion.

Printed invitations for a Naming Ceremony are available but can be hard to find. Alternatively you could make your own invitations, or perhaps write a brief letter. If you have older children it

Top Tip!

If you don't want your guests to feel obliged to bring formal gifts – perhaps because they did so recently (after the birth) – you could suggest something symbolic; a donation to a children's charity, or a book or something they've made. There are more suggestions in the chapter entitled 'Ideas and themes'.

could be a fun project to help them feel involved. The most important things to include, starting with the most obvious, are:

- What the event is
- Who it's for
- When it's taking place (day, date, time)
- Where it's taking place
- What it will involve

It's vital everyone knows what time to arrive to avoid holding up the start of the ceremony. You might think it's worthwhile 'fixing' the time to ensure nobody turns up late. If the ceremony's due to start at 3pm there's no harm in stating 2:30pm on the invitation! It's also worth including a sketch map of the venue, and the post code for guests who want to get a map online or use a satellite navigation device.

Most people are pretty good at responding promptly to invitations, but an RSVP is still a good idea, maybe followed with '…. by (date) please'. And because many of your guests won't know what to expect it's a good idea to pen a brief note to include with the invitation that will help them visualise the event. Maybe something like this, adapted to your own purposes:

Dear James and Alison,

We'd be (honoured / thrilled / pleased) if you would join us for this important event to celebrate the birth of (name).

We decided to have a Naming Ceremony because (we feel it's a very personal and meaningful way for us to welcome (name) into our family). It'll be a very special day for us so we'll be dressed (accordingly / in our Sunday best / smart but casual). Just so you can time your arrival, the ceremony itself is due to start at (2.30pm).

After the ceremony there'll be a (BBQ / formal dinner / buffet / light lunch) and (music / a disco / fireworks / garden games / children's entertainment / a fun surprise).

Leading the ceremony

As with any kind of ceremony the person leading it is its lynch pin, providing structure and flow and guiding everyone seamlessly through all its stages. Who you choose to lead your ceremony is, of course, entirely up to you but there are three clear options:

Leading it yourself

This is possible, but it's tricky and it's not an option which will be suitable for many parents.

- You are key to the ceremony and wearing two different 'hats' is very challenging
- You'll have so much to do on the day that the additional pressure of leading the ceremony might just be too much
- You might become more emotional than you anticipate and the ceremony could suffer as a result

All in all, you will find the day much more relaxing if the ceremony is led by someone else.

Top Tip!

What the ceremony leader wears will have a great impact on the tone of the ceremony. If a friend's doing it you'll probably want them to dress for the occasion, even if you're aiming for an informal event. If appropriate, they could always slip into something more informal after the ceremony itself. A good way of establishing what's acceptable is to tell the ceremony leader what you'll be wearing.

Asking someone you know

If you ask someone you know to lead the ceremony for you, make sure they really are comfortable doing it and that they have experience of this type of public speaking. Giving a business presentation is very different from an informal but dignified event like this.

However, he or she doesn't need to be a witty after-dinner speaker as you might look for in, say, a best man. It's important, though, that they genuinely understand what the ceremony means to you and will set the right tone.

If you know someone who fits the bill, and they agree to do it for you, make sure you get the script to them as early as you can so they can practise it. Make sure they won't promote their own philosophy or beliefs, or add witty asides – this is your ceremony and they will need to stick to the script.

Top Tip!
Ask your ceremony leader to use some kind of presentation folder. Having loose papers looks unprofessional and they can easily be dropped (or blow around if you're outside).

You could ask two people to each perform one part of the ceremony, which works fine as long as it's clear which of them is conducting each part.

Finally, have a back–up plan. Choose someone who would step in at the last minute to lead the ceremony if some unforeseen emergency prevents your chosen ceremony leader from attending.

A professional Celebrant

Having a professional Celebrant guarantees that your ceremony will be exactly that – professional from start to finish. You'll be in contact with the Celebrant before the event, so you can talk it through and make sure everything's going to be exactly as you want it to be.

A professional Celebrant will be smart and tidy, will arrive in good time, cope with any last minute changes and conduct the ceremony according to your wishes, guiding you seamlessly through it from beginning to end.

Your Celebrant's primary goal is to ensure that your ceremony runs smoothly and that you have a truly memorable day.

Shortly after the ceremony the Celebrant will discreetly slip away, leaving you to enjoy the rest of your day with your guests. It costs around £100 to £160 to have a professional Celebrant. You'll find that it's money well spent.

Our survey said...

We asked parents who used a professional Celebrant from Civil Ceremonies Ltd what they thought...

" The Celebrant was organised and calm and allayed all our concerns.

She was brilliant and the day ran smoothly and efficiently; very professional throughout.

The Celebrant was great; very organised and polite, the ceremony ran smoothly because of her.

He was very good and helpful; thought of things that we hadn't.

The experience was excellent - very professional; she was open to our suggestions.

He was very nice to talk to and conducted the ceremony in a professional manner. He was great; did a fantastic job.

We could not be happier – she made everyone feel relaxed.

The whole day revolved around us as a family – it was all really personal. "

Laura and John have held two Naming Ceremonies; one for their son Sam in 2006 and another for their daughter Scarlett in 2008. They share their experiences with us in their own words.

Neither John or I are religious so we felt it wasn't right to use the church just for our own benefit for the purpose of Christening our children. But it would be unfair if, feeling this way, our children couldn't enjoy a ceremony that welcomes them into all our lives and indeed to this world. A Naming Ceremony ticked all the boxes for us. It allowed us to have a proper ceremony in which we could choose the equivalent of godparents and in which we could reaffirm, in support of our feelings for our children, what were essentially our wedding vows.

Both our children's Naming Ceremonies have meant the world to us. We spent a lot of time choosing the promises very carefully, and a lot of time and effort went into every aspect of it – from choosing the venue, deciding which friends and family members we felt were most appropriate to be their Supporting Adults, to choosing Sam's and Scarlett's little outfits.

We worked closely with our Celebrant to make sure all details were perfect for the day itself. And the ceremony was, in a word, beautiful. The venue was idyllic and the Celebrant, Caroline, was just wonderful – very patient and friendly and well spoken.

If we had another ceremony we would definitely have a Celebrant again. Having a Celebrant to guide us through the ceremony and the weeks leading up to the actual day was superb.

She made our first ceremony, for Sam, so very special that we later asked her to perform Scarlett's.

The promises we chose were very appropriate for the way we feel about our children. They are things we would do for our children anyway – love them unconditionally and support them in all the choices they make, and try to guide them in life. But to be able to say them all out loud in front of the most important people in our lives just made it a wonderful experience for everyone.

Our Supporting Adults were John's aunt and uncle. They know what it's like to have children and we felt their life experience would serve Scarlett well in her future life. I know they feel the same way about Sam, too, and it does seem to have brought our families a lot closer. They said they thought the promises were all very appropriate, well thought out and wonderfully delivered by the Celebrant. A lovely way to demonstrate the recognition of a child and to make a commitment to their little lives.

Many of our friends came away from the day saying they thought it was delightful. It has even prompted them to consider doing something similar for their own children. Some of the older generation, it's fair to say, were dubious about having a Naming Ceremony rather than a traditional Christening. But having seen and heard how heartfelt the promises were, coupled with the

very real sense of a dignified ceremony, they came away with a very different attitude. We saw more than a few tears amongst them so the vows were obviously touching some heartstrings!

We are lucky to have our perfect pigeon pair – our Sam and little Scarlett. Sam's ceremony was at Marwell Zoo – he is our own little monkey! Scarlett's was in the gardens at Jermyns House – her name is Scarlett Rose so we felt a beautiful garden was most appropriate. At both ceremonies we had afternoon teas, with sandwiches and scones – very civilised! We all had such a wonderful time.

If we had another ceremony we would definitely have a Celebrant again. Having a Celebrant to guide us through the ceremony and the weeks leading up to the actual day was superb. Thank you so much Caroline!

Looking back now, we feel that a Naming Ceremony has been even more personal than a traditional Christening as all aspects of it were chosen by us. I would highly recommend a Naming Ceremony to anyone who wants to mark their child's arrival into this world but doesn't feel a religious ceremony is appropriate. Just such a beautiful day for everyone – hardly a dry eye in the house – lovely.

Laura & John Clough
Hampshire

Key roles

Your older children

If you have older children you'll probably want to involve them as much as you can; partly because you don't want them to feel left out but also because it's a great way of acknowledging the important role they'll play in their younger sibling's life. If they're reluctant to be 'named' during the ceremony, due to their age, having them read a brief poem – perhaps even one they've written themselves – makes for a wonderfully poignant moment. They could also make their own promise to be a good brother or sister, or play a role in one of the many symbolic gestures that could follow the ceremony (see the chapter entitled *'Ideas and themes'*).

Supporting Adults

Choosing the right Supporting Adults is, of course, extremely important as they'll develop a very special bond with your child. They'll be people you trust to provide a good and positive influence, and who'll see him or her regularly.

They'll certainly be from your 'inner circle' of close friends and family, although if the child has no natural grandparents you might consider it important to include an older couple.

When they're introduced to everyone the Celebrant could also explain why they've been chosen.

Just so you know . . .

A ceremony should include the signing of a certificate which is then presented to the parents as a permanent record of the ceremony. Special certificates for Supporting Adults and grandparents are also available from www.civilceremonies.co.uk

During the ceremony they'll make special promises of ongoing love and support; promises they need to be comfortable with and confident of upholding. It's a good idea to discuss exactly what you hope for from the people you choose, and to discuss the nature of the promises they'll be making.

Those promises could be to simply keep in touch with the child and take an active interest in his or her progress, and to provide love and support in the years ahead. Or you could also include specific promises that relate to a Supporting Adult's talents, vocation or special experience.

Grandparents

Grandparents are sometimes unsure about a Naming Ceremony, as a Christening was probably traditional when their children were young. However, some of our best feedback comes from grandparents who approach us after a ceremony, overwhelmed by how touching and personal it was.

In the ceremony the wording used for grandparents usually involves them promising to continue to support the

family, as they've done in the past, and to give the baby their love and support as well as their experience of life.

Do involve grandparents if you can; they need not say anything if they don't want to, but their support can certainly be acknowledged.

Other family and friends

Whether they're Supporting Adults or not, friends and family will be touched and honoured to be asked to read something at the ceremony. Although they may have some trepidation about speaking in public it does make the ceremony much more personal and meaningful to have someone read a poem. Try not to give anyone sleepless nights – show them the type of readings you have in mind. Bear in mind that it's probably not a good idea to surprise them with something on the day – or to let them surprise you!

Key roles

Top Tip!

If a family member has had a baby at a similar time it might make sense to have a ceremony for both babies on the same day when all the family can get together. However, because the content of each ceremony is very personal, and those with key roles in the ceremony will probably be different, the two ceremonies should be separate; held one after the other.

If you have friends who have had a baby at a similar time, don't be tempted to combine the event as it will detract from the personal nature of the ceremony and you will end up sharing the event with their relatives, many of whom will be strangers to you.

Planning your
ceremony

As you've seen in the preceding pages, your ceremony will include many different elements. Let's now look at the most usual core ceremony features in their logical sequence to see how the ceremony comes together.

Welcome

The Celebrant opens the ceremony with words of welcome for you and your guests. This might be followed by a brief introduction to the universal tradition of having a ceremony to mark the birth of a child. It's a good idea to also have a few words about the concept of Naming Ceremonies in particular, and your own reasons for holding one. Some of your guests won't have been to one before and this will help them to appreciate the importance of the occasion to you, and help them understand what's going to happen during the ceremony.

Readings

This is an ideal moment to involve one of your family members or friends by having them read an appropriate poem. It could be something they've written as a special dedication to your child, or a favourite poem of yours.

Selections of suitable readings are available from professional ceremony providers. You could choose anything, from the formal to the sublime; from the traditional to something more light-hearted. It's a good idea to choose two or three contrasting styles and have them read at intervals during the ceremony.

An example of poetry that sets the scene for a Naming Ceremony very aptly is 'Meditation on the Upbringing of Children'.

To lighten the mood later in the ceremony you might want to include something a little more whimsical. '(Baby), my son/daughter' and 'Night, night mummy; see you later' are two very popular examples.

'Meditation on the Upbringing of Children' by Dorothy Louise-Law Nolte

If children live with criticism, they learn to condemn;
If children live with hostility, they learn how to fight;
If children live with ridicule, they learn to be shy;
If children live with shame, they learn to feel guilty.

If children live with tolerance, they learn to be patient;
If children live with encouragement, they learn to have confidence;
If children live with praise, they learn to appreciate;
If children live with fairness, they learn justice.

If children live with security, they learn to have faith;
If children live with approval, they learn to like themselves;
If children live with love around them, they learn to give love to the world.

'(Baby), my son/daughter' by Andy Ballantyne

Ten wee fingers, ten tiny toes
Bright shining eyes and a wee button nose
Huge healthy lungs and soft downy hair
A miracle we wanted all the world to share

When you have a child you see things in a different light
You second guess yourself, hoping you're always right
In the early decisions you have to be strong
Hoping and praying you do nothing wrong

We'll kiss him/her and hug him/her and give lots of tender care
This miracle, this boy/girl, depends on us being there
Our love for him/her is something that can never be measured
Our (baby), my son/daughter, who will always be treasured

'Night night, Mummy; see you Later' Anonymous

At seven o'clock every evening my Mum tucks me up in my bed
I'm nice and snug in my 'jamas beside me my faithful old Ted.

I always nod off very quickly - before Mum has turned out the light,
But when it's her bedtime much later, well then I wake up for the night.

For there's no time of day I like better than the hours between midnight and three,
For Mum hasn't got any housework and can give her attention to me.

And when I start yelling and shouting, Mum knows that she has to be quick
For the night when she leaves me to grizzle is the night I decide to be sick.

But Mum can't mind in the slightest at being my playmate 'til two -
She'd normally spend this time sleeping, for she's nothing much better to do.

Some nights she mixes a cocktail from the bottles she keeps on the shelf,
Which sometimes she gives me to swallow and sometimes she gulps down herself!

And if in the morning I'm sleepy and feel in the need of a perk,
I can have forty winks in my pushchair while Mummy gets on with her work.

But nothing's as nice as the night time. And nothing can equal the pleasure
Of finding it's four in the morning and being Mum's wide-awake treasure.

Naming of the child

The Celebrant says a few words to introduce this part of the ceremony and then asks you to confirm your child's full name.

If there's a personal significance to the name or names you've chosen, you might like to use this opportunity to share those reasons with your assembled guests.

This is also a good time for a guest or the Celebrant to offer an inspirational reading or blessing. Again, this could be something you've written yourself or one taken from a book of poetry or verse. The most popular theme for a reading like this is something that expresses your hopes for your child's future.

Parents' promises

Your public declarations of love and support are probably the most important part of the entire ceremony. The promises you make are very personal and meaningful, and reflect the kind of parent you're undertaking to be.

The actual wording is a personal choice. Most parents focus on the great responsibility of being a parent and how they'll offer their child respect, tolerance, honesty, kindness, humour and their unconditional love and protection.

You might choose just one or two promises; simply saying you'll be the best parent you can be (like the examples shown below), or you could choose a whole range of promises that reflect specific ways in which you'll positively influence your child's life.

Here are examples of promises you might want to include:

We promise to keep Sarah safe and clothe her, shelter and protect her, love and support her for as long as she needs us, to the very best of our ability.

We will encourage and support Chloe in her chosen endeavours, irrespective of success or failure; encourage her to express her own thoughts and feelings without fear of rejection and teach her moral values to enable her to become a responsible and caring adult.

We will endeavour to bring Martin up in a home filled with love and kindness, and teach him to have tolerance for others and respect for humanity and the earth which supports us.

A vow to each other

Many parents find the ceremony to be a very emotional occasion and also a highly poignant moment in their life together. This can make it an ideal opportunity to also make promises to each other.

This could be an affirmation of the key vows you made when you married, or it could be a completely new vow specifically relating to the upbringing of your child. If you aren't married it might be a promise of commitment to each other to guarantee stability in your child's life.

Whatever vow or vows you choose to make, you'll find that doing so enhances both the atmosphere of the ceremony and the binding and intimate nature of it as a whole.

Parents' address

In addition to making promises to the child and, perhaps, to each other, many parents like to say a few words about what being a parent means to them and how it's influenced their lives. This could be especially relevant if your child was conceived in special circumstances, like with the help of IVF, for example.

It could just be that parenthood has had a significant impact on your outlook or has changed your lifestyle priorities. People who know you may have noticed the effect parenthood has had on you, and this is your opportunity to share your innermost feelings.

An 'address' needn't be in the form of a 'reading' – it could simply be a sentence or two about how you now look afresh at life and how the experience had caused you to re-assess what's really important.

Supporting adults' promises

Here, the Celebrant introduces another vital element of the ceremony. As we've discussed, the Supporting Adults you choose will have an extremely important role in your child's life. Their public declarations of ongoing love and support can be either just to the child or perhaps to the family as a whole. Again, the promises you choose will be personal to you and it's important that your Supporting Adults are comfortable about making those promises. Discuss the content with them in advance and decide who will promise what.

It's usual for the Celebrant to read out the selected promises to the appropriate Supporting Adults in turn and for them to respond 'I promise'.

Here are some examples of the kind of promises you might choose to include:

> Do you promise that in times of difficulty, Darren and Julia, and their son Matthew, can turn to you for reassurance and help?
>
> Do you promise to keep careful watch over Bethany until she grows to be an adult and to always be ready to advise, encourage and comfort her?
>
> Will you promise to take time to get to know Jonathan and keep in touch with him while he's growing up?

Grandparents' promises

The special bond between a child and his or her grandparents can also be acknowledged in the ceremony. Grandparents play an important role in a child's life and may want to publicly share their own thoughts and feelings. If they'd rather not make a formal speech, they could simply respond to a brief promise of support delivered by the Celebrant.

Involving other family members

If your child has older siblings you could involve them in the ceremony by having them promise to love and protect their baby brother or sister.

If they're old enough you could ask them to write a few words of their own about what having a baby brother or sister means to them. Alternatively they could simply answer a resounding "Yes!" to a brief question put to them by the Celebrant.

However you choose to involve them, your older children will appreciate being made to feel an important part of the ceremony.

Absent guests

If someone important to you is unable to attend the ceremony you could read out a message on their behalf, or have the Celebrant do it for you.

However, if someone close to you has recently died the question of using the occasion to pay tribute to them might cause you a dilemma. Of course, you'll not want to make a happy occasion sad, but the person leading the ceremony should be able to use appropriate wording at the right time to enable you to remember them, without affecting the overall mood.

Try to create an appropriate interlude when your guests will be attentive but which doesn't immediately follow a light-hearted reading, for example. After a respectful pause the Celebrant will continue with the rest of the ceremony.

A special gift

A special gift to your child can be presented during the ceremony. Gifts provided by your guests would normally be opened later, but there may be something significant – whether something handed down through the family or something personal, perhaps that you've had specially made – that you want to have opened in front of everyone.

Closing the ceremony

Most ceremonies feature a further reading at this point, after which the Celebrant brings the ceremony to a close. The closing is the end of the formal part of the ceremony but is normally closely followed by other closing actions.

The closing words themselves usually consist of a blessing and/or a reiteration of the importance of the ceremony and an invitation to enjoy the rest of the day. This could be delivered solely by the Celebrant or he or she could deliver the closing words and then invite you to add a few words of your own.

Certificates

The Celebrant should provide you with a certificate as a permanent record of the ceremony. Either presented at the close of the ceremony, or given to you afterwards if you prefer, the certificate is your own personal keepsake that reiterates the special promises you've made. Special certificates for Supporting Adults and grandparents can also be signed as a lasting reminder of their pledges.

Symbolic presentations

As well as proposing a toast, there are many special actions you can perform to highlight the close of the ceremony before everyone disperses to enjoy the rest of the day.

For example, you could plant a tree or bury a time-capsule. You could also light a candle or release balloons or fireworks.

For further ideas and suggestions for enhancing the occasion see the chapter entitled 'Ideas and themes'.

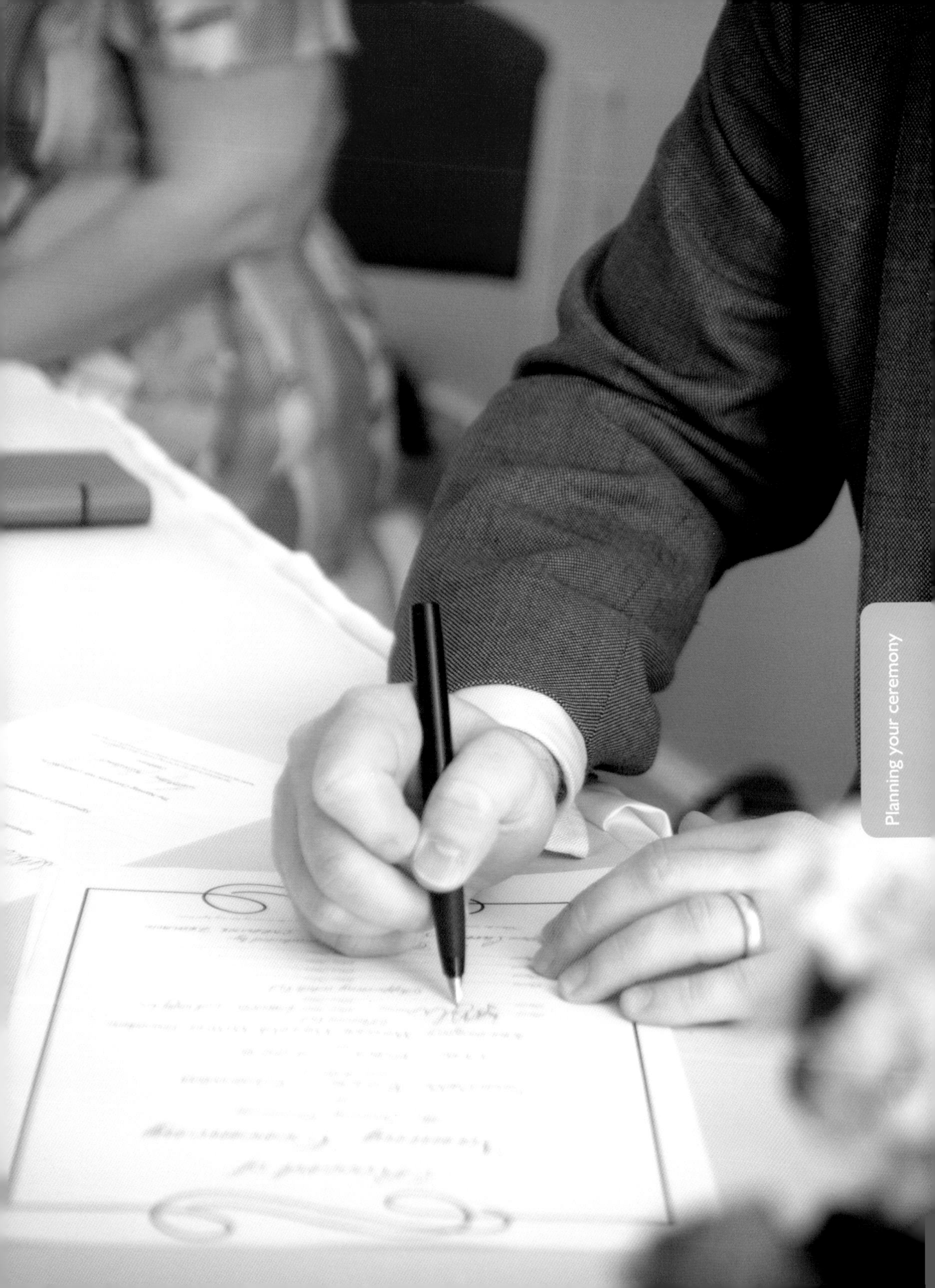

Special ceremonies

There are specific ceremonies for which special wording or an amended version of the standard ceremony structure might be required.

Adopted children

A Naming Ceremony is an excellent choice for adoptive parents to celebrate the new addition to their family. It's an especially appropriate celebration for the long-awaited end to the legal adoption process and is also a great opportunity for the wider circle of family and friends to share this happy and momentous event.

If the child has lived with the family for a considerable time, the ceremony may take on even more importance, especially if the adoption has also resulted in a change of name. It's a public recognition of the new legal status of the child and the absolute commitment of the family to him or her.

Adoption increasingly involves older children rather than babies, and your ceremony will need to reflect this. The older the child, the greater the need to consult him or her about the content of the ceremony.

Extra thought needs to be given about the choice of Supporting Adults and the type of promises they'll make. It could be that you'll choose fewer Supporting Adults but that they'll be people who gave you particular support during the adoption process, and who created a special bond with the child from early on.

> We didn't give you the gift of life, but in our hearts we know the love we feel is as deep and real as if it had been so. For us to have each other is like a dream come true. No — we didn't give you the gift of life; life gave us the gift of you.

Step-children

A high percentage of adoptions are step-child adoptions. Whether or not the child is being officially adopted by the new parent will influence the wording you choose for the ceremony. It could be that the term 'Naming Ceremony' isn't appropriate and you may decide to call it a 'Welcoming' instead, or simply a Family Celebration.

A ceremony to embrace a step-child can be a particularly emotional time, especially for the child. He or she may be of an age where an in-depth discussion about the content of the ceremony is necessary. Older children will have their own views about what should be said and what should happen, and those views will need to be taken into account.

Following a wedding or other ceremony

Five percent of all Naming Ceremonies are held on the same day as a wedding. Others take place after a legal Civil Partnership Ceremony, or a Commitment Ceremony. These are ceremonies undertaken by same-sex couples or couples who don't wish to get married but still want a public declaration of their commitment to each other.

Where children exist in a relationship, holding a Naming Ceremony immediately after their legal marriage (or other ceremony) appeals to many couples. It's a natural extension of their own decision to 'tie the knot' in the way that's appropriate to them, and is a logical choice because family and friends are already gathered together.

Most Register Offices can now host a Naming Ceremony after a legal marriage (or Civil Partnership Ceremony) in the same room. It may not be the same person who conducts both ceremonies.

Alternatively, you could hold the Naming Ceremony at a different location (the reception venue, for example) to keep the ceremonies entirely separate.

For some married couples, the family gathering for a Naming Ceremony provides them with the opportunity to hold a full Renewal of Marriage Vows ceremony. This particularly appeals when the Naming Ceremony coincides with a significant wedding anniversary. A professional Celebrant can conduct both ceremonies, either with a short break between them or with one flowing into the other.

A special birthday

Your child's first few birthdays are all magical. You witness many amazing changes as he or she progresses from baby to toddler, developing a unique personality and individuality as the months and years go by. Each of these early birthdays are significant, but none more so that your child's first birthday. Little wonder that many parents choose to hold a Naming Ceremony at this very special milestone.

A special birthday Naming Ceremony is a wonderful event, and is enhanced further when the ceremony script is crafted to reflect the occasion. Special wording within the script helps to combine these two celebrations into one exceptionally joyful event. You can inject this personalisation throughout the ceremony, or simply refer to the birthday in one or two sections, such as the Naming and Parents' Promises.

If you are planning to use a professional ceremony provider they will help you develop a unique and very special birthday naming script.

As well as amended wording to reflect the occasion you might also want to include a poem in the ceremony that particularly reflects the significance of the day.

A good example is the following:

My First Birthday

Just 12 short months ago I made my big debut
So now I'd like to celebrate my 1st Birthday with you.

My little hands play pat-a-cake, they peek-a-boo and wave.....
They catch me while I learn to walk and splash me as I bathe.

They hold your fingers tightly and touch your heart so deep.
My little hands reach out to you for hugs before I sleep.

My little hands are tiny now but yours will serve to guide me.
And when I'm grown I'll still reach out and know you're right beside me.

Special ceremonies

A Christmas ceremony

Many ceremonies are held at special times of the year, such as at Easter or at Christmas time. This is partly because it's often easier to bring together a widely-spread family during national holidays, but it's also because the ceremony can take on added significance, or simply be enhanced, by the holiday-event itself.

Again, special wording in the ceremony script can associate the Naming Ceremony with the 'new birth' aspect of Easter or the spiritual significance of Christmas. There are also many ways you can use the holiday period to add a theme to the ceremony, either decoratively or with symbolic actions. An egg-hunt, for example, would be a fun way to keep guests involved after an Easter ceremony, and could take on added significance by attaching messages to the eggs. These could simply be a 'thank you' from your child that will help give the other children (and their parents) fond memories of the day.

Children who are ill or who have special needs

If you have a child who has a serious medical condition, tell the Celebrant about it so he or she can ensure the structure of the ceremony takes account of any special requirements.

It may be that you'll want the ceremony to be exactly as it would be for any other child, without any distinction whatsoever. On the other hand there may be certain aspects of the ceremony where you want special wording to be included.

An ill parent

Sometimes a ceremony is a particularly poignant occasion because a parent is seriously ill. In these circumstances the ceremony is often held, not so much to celebrate a Naming, but to specifically put in place a publicly declared network of support. The parents want to make sure their children have the promised support of family and friends in case anything happens to them, and in this way provide reassurance and stability at a difficult and uncertain time for the family.

A ceremony in these circumstances will be particularly emotional and the wording will need very careful thought. The assistance of a professional Celebrant will be invaluable, and he or she will ensure the ceremony is exactly as you want it.

A ceremony like this is often arranged on the parents' behalf by close family and friends.

Getting it right
on the day

Probably the most important consideration is deciding who will write the ceremony. You might decide that the whole thing is too onerous and time-consuming to write yourself, and that's where a professionally written ceremony script comes in. If you want the whole thing to be easy and stress-free, then without doubt the best way is to have a professional ceremony provider create the script (to your own personal requirements) and to have the ceremony delivered by a professional Celebrant.

However, that's not to say you can't do it yourself. Certainly, with the help of this book, you can. And if you've got a very good idea about exactly what you want to say you'll be off to a good start.

Writing the script yourself

Writing a Naming Ceremony is very different from writing a presentation or a speech. For one thing it's not a monologue; the person leading the ceremony will be introducing each section but will prompt interaction from the various key players and readers.

What you write needs to sound right when it's read out loud. Often a sentence looks fine on paper but can sound laboured or disjointed when read to an audience. You also need to avoid embarrassing pauses, so it's important to make notations in the script so the person leading it knows where people should stand, and who should speak, for each part of the ceremony.

The key to a ceremony that's relaxing and stress-free for all involved is effective planning and preparation. When writing the script bear in mind these six key points:

- Maintain a logical structure
- Avoid long words
- Keep sentences short
- Type double-spaced and in large lettering
- Read it all aloud to check it flows smoothly
- Walk the whole ceremony through

Top Tip!
A ceremony generally lasts between 20 and 30 minutes, depending on how much you choose to include. A ceremony with a great deal of content could last up to an hour.

Choosing readings

We've already discussed the types of poetry and other readings you might like to include in the ceremony, but it's worth mentioning here that a lot of people DREAD reading in public. Make sure you choose pieces that the readers will feel at ease delivering. Pieces by Shakespeare or Yeats, for example, can trip up even eloquent readers!

Of course, some people are natural public speakers. If one or two of your guests share that trait they'll obviously be ideal choices. The fall-back position is the professional Celebrant, who will be experienced in public speaking and will be used to delivering this type of poetry or prose.

The star of the show

It's ideal if everyone can sit throughout the ceremony, but in some situations this may not be practical. What's important, though, is that everyone has a good view of the star of the show – your child.

You'll almost certainly want to be seated to the side of the table at which the Celebrant conducts the ceremony, facing your guests. The other key players in the ceremony should be (preferably seated) in the front row of guests. From here they can quickly and easily take their positions when called upon during the ceremony.

If possible, arrange seating in a semi-circular or staggered configuration as this helps to avoid taller guests blocking the view of others.

It's also a good idea to have the top table at the opposite end of the room from the entrance. This allows any latecomers to slip into the back without disturbing the proceedings.

A word about movement

Allow enough space for your key players to move into position without them having to ask others to make way. When it comes to introducing your Supporting Adults, bear in mind that saying nice things about them while they're seated is far less embarrassing for them than doing so once they've stood up! Keep a supply of tissues handy, too, as moist eyes are very likely and it saves guests searching in pockets and handbags.

Preparing the table

The table is used for signing the certificates. A professional Celebrant will provide a certificate for you, but if someone you know is leading the ceremony you'll need to provide one. If you want to present Supporting Adults or grandparents with a certificate you'll also need to obtain these for whoever is leading the ceremony.

You can also use the table to display a special cake, naming day candles, your special gift and perhaps a flower display. Decorating the table with naming day banners and balloons is also very popular.

If you're having the ceremony outside make sure you have some paperweights. It's also a good idea to put any candles inside glass vases to avoid them blowing out.

Getting it right on the day

Disturbances

Almost everyone carries a mobile phone these days. But since there's nothing worse than a jaunty ring-tone blasting out just as you're making emotional promises of love to your child, make sure the person leading the ceremony asks everyone to ensure phones are turned off before the ceremony starts. A professional Celebrant will do this automatically.

If something unexpected happens during the ceremony a Celebrant will wait for the disturbance to pass and then carry on. There's nothing you can do about a fire engine hurtling past, but you can take steps to avoid many other potential disturbances.

If you're having the ceremony at home it's wise to lock pets away during the proceedings as they can get excited and cause disruption. Turn the house phone off, too, and have someone monitor the front door in case any canvassers decide to come knocking. It's also a good idea to warn neighbours about all the extra cars, and to ask those closest to avoid mowing the grass, lighting bonfires or playing loud music.

Your baby

It can all be a bit overwhelming for a young baby and it's possible this could translate into a tearful episode. Don't worry if your baby starts crying – it's best just to signal the Celebrant that you want to pause for a few minutes and use that time to get baby settled again.

If your child won't be placated, and you've passed the point in the ceremony where the baby is named, you could always have a guest take the baby outside for a while so you can continue. One way to minimise the chances of this occurring is to time the ceremony around your baby's normal routine so he or she is fed and rested.

Photography

You will doubtless want a good selection of photographs of the entire day. However, having several heads bobbing up and down - and countless flashes going off - during the ceremony can be very intrusive indeed.

There are bound to be a few budding photographers among your guests, with good quality digital cameras. So for the ceremony itself, why not consider appointing two of them (for luck) as your 'official' photographers? You can give them a list of the most important shots you want.

There are many good websites where you can create an online album free of charge for all your guests to visit, or they can email the choicest photos around. This might not discourage all your guests from taking photos during the ceremony, but it will probably limit it. This can also be a great way to encourage your guests to keep in touch with each other after the event.

A video of the event also makes a great keepsake and, again, those with digital camcorders will be more than happy to share their photography skills with you – and everyone else if asked!

Setting the scene

Creating just the right atmosphere for the ceremony may prove the most difficult thing of all if you are not using a professional Celebrant. If someone you know is leading it for you, they'll need to assertively (but not in a sergeant-major fashion!) get everyone's attention and welcome them. Much will depend upon how formal you wish the ceremony to be and the setting you choose.

Late arrivals

Traffic these days can challenge even the best-prepared of us. But rest assured that only a genuine unforeseen emergency will prevent a professional Celebrant arriving in good time for your ceremony, and they'll have a back-up plan for most eventualities.

However, your Celebrant probably won't be able to delay the start of a ceremony by more than half an hour for late arrivals so it's vital that your invitations emphasise the importance of arriving in good time.

If a key player has phoned ahead to say they can't get there for the start of the ceremony you could rearrange the sequence to give them extra time. If they can't get there before the ceremony is due to finish you'll just have to press on without them.

If they were due to deliver a reading the Celebrant will read it for them. If they're one of your Supporting Adults, for example, you may need to simply have the Celebrant read out their promises in their absence.

Postponement

What happens if you or the baby falls ill and you have no choice but to postpone the ceremony?

If you do need to postpone, most companies, including professional ceremony providers and venues, will be sympathetic and simply rearrange your booking.

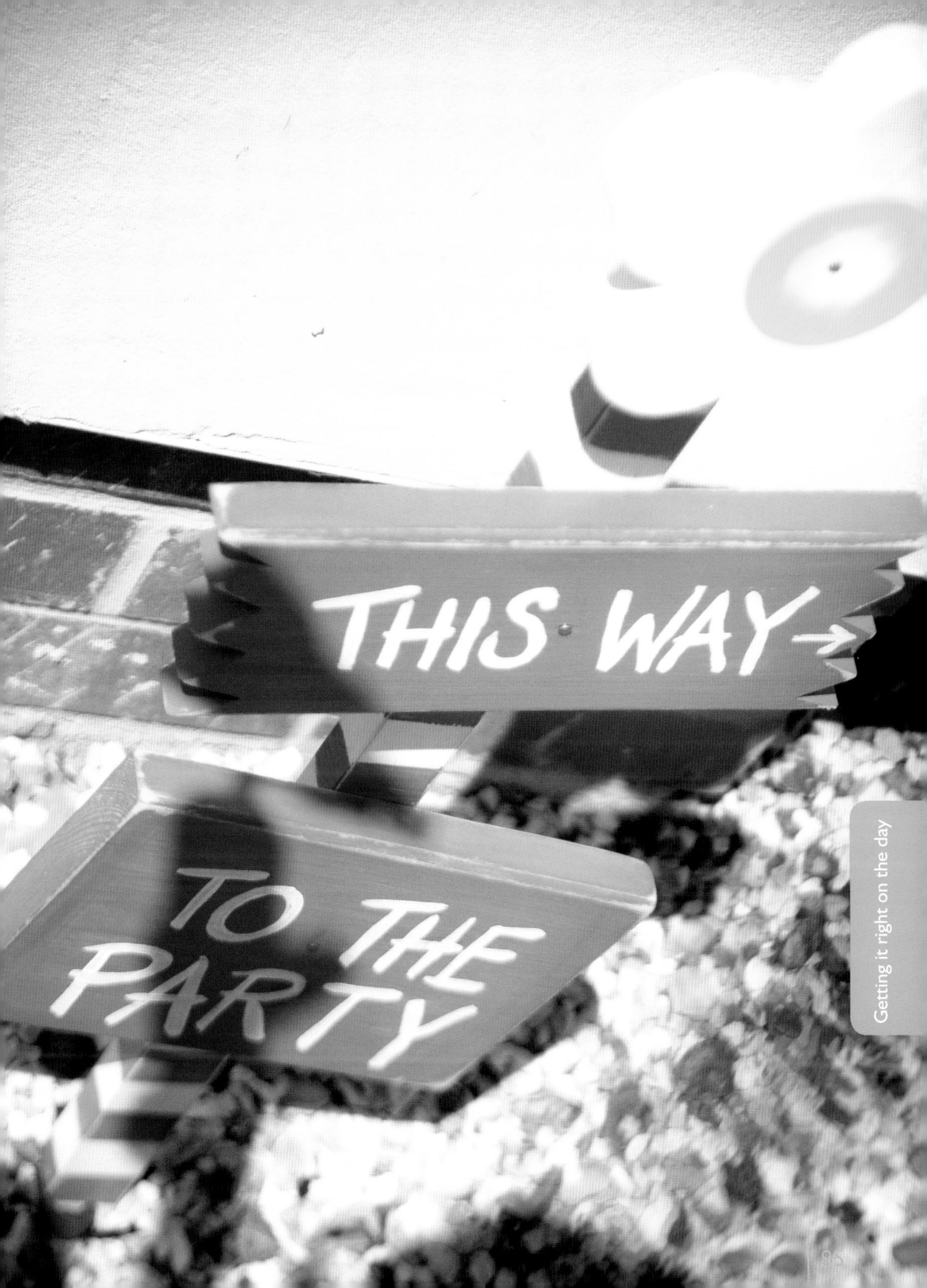
THIS WAY →
TO THE
PARTY

Amber's parents wanted her extended family to not just be witnesses to a ceremony, but to be an integral part of it and for it to be the inspiration for their involvement in Amber's future life.

We chose to have a Naming Ceremony to welcome Amber into the family because it was a wonderful opportunity for everyone from both sides of the family to meet her. We managed to get everyone from our big extended families in one place and felt this was a fantastic way to celebrate. For us it was a straightforward decision to have a non-religious ceremony, as neither of us is religious. However, we wanted to have a ceremony into which we could have a major input.

We felt the ceremony was a way of welcoming the most precious person into our lives. We were able to choose our own words to really express ourselves and it was especially important to be able to include our dads, who each delivered their choice of reading for us.

> The ceremony itself was exceptional; everyone that was special to us was able to meet and welcome our very special baby girl and the ceremony seemed to cement the bond for us and make us even more complete.

We had family travelling from all over the country and the traffic was really bad. We had a lot of people that had not arrived but the Celebrant waited until everyone who was special to us had arrived.

The ceremony itself was exceptional; everyone that was special to us was able to meet and welcome our very special baby girl and the ceremony seemed to cement the bond for us and make us even more complete. After the actual ceremony we were able to spend valuable time with our family and friends and to allow Amber time with her new family.

As all the people that were invited to the ceremony are special supporting people to us we wanted all of them to be special people in Amber's life. For this reason we decided not to name specific Supporting Adults but rather asked everyone there to be a Supporting Adult in Amber's life. We felt this involved everyone in a very special way, and Amber is able to start her life knowing that she has a large support network behind her.

All our guests were very complimentary about the ceremony and the sentiments behind the words and readings. Everyone seemed to really enjoy the afternoon. We decided on a Celebrant because we wanted all our family and friends to enjoy the ceremony and be a guest for the day. We felt the Celebrant really made the ceremony for us – she was interested in us, and in Amber, and had the compassion and understanding when our guests were stuck in traffic. The Celebrant had obviously taken a lot of time preparing for the ceremony and her personal attention made the day extra special. On our next Naming Ceremony we would definitely have a Celebrant again.

We held the ceremony at a local hotel. We were able to hire the room for the ceremony and then the hotel changed the room for us to have a buffet, cake and speeches. We decorated the room with balloons, banners and confetti. All in all, it was a really wonderful day.

David & Nicola Jaques
Milton Keynes

Ideas and themes

Some of the ideas and themes for enhancing your ceremony have already been hinted at in previous chapters. Here, though, we take a closer look at many of those ideas and give you some useful guidance to make them work successfully. First, though, let's look at the various catering options, some of which will be obvious but others, perhaps, less so.

At a venue

Depending on what time you have your ceremony there are lots of options for providing your guests with refreshments. For obvious reasons, it's best to offer food after the ceremony has taken place.

At a hotel, you could provide a light lunch if the ceremony takes place in the morning, or 'high tea' with sandwiches and cake mid-late afternoon. If you're planning evening entertainment you'll also need to consider what food to offer later on. This doesn't have to mean providing a four-course meal; a finger buffet is a good choice and needn't be particularly expensive. Bear in mind that if refreshments are being provided in the same room as the ceremony, staff will need time to rearrange the room and set it up ready for the food.

How all of this fits into your budget is an obvious consideration. One way of limiting your expenditure is to restrict your offering to food only (plus tea and coffee). Bar bills can easily get out of hand!

If you take over a favourite restaurant you could agree a deal with the proprietor to offer a limited number of main courses at a special price. The certainty of what they're providing

makes things a whole lot easier and more cost-effective for them. A friendly owner will probably also agree a special deal for wine; after all, they're getting a guaranteed 'full house'.

Other venues, like a village hall, should allow you to do your own catering, which is obviously less expensive. Check that they have a license for the consumption of alcohol on the premises.

At home

Having the ceremony at home does, of course, give you total control over the costs. One thing to bear in mind, though, is that unless asked most guests probably won't bring a bottle as they might for an ordinary party. If you don't want guests to feel obliged to contribute, it's good to know that you can easily provide wine, beer and soft drinks for a quarter of the price you'd pay from a bar. And providing even an elaborate buffet needn't break the bank.

In the garden

Having the ceremony in the garden gives you further options for providing food and drink.

A barbecue is a great way to round of the day, and it's perfectly acceptable to ask guests to contribute by bringing a bottle. Another way of limiting the expense is to have a communal picnic, allocating different guests to bring salads, cold meats, fish, cheeses and quiches while you provide the hot food and a range of breads, pickles, etc.

Decorating the venue

One easy way to add colour and help make the event special is to decorate the venue with pink or blue themed "Happy Naming Day" balloons, banners and ribbons. Some items can also be bought personalised for extra effect. Flowers, too, add a splash of colour. There are all sorts of other themed products you can use to good effect, like Naming Day napkins.

Another idea is to display photographs from the birth – well, perhaps not the

actual birth – right up to the present day so guests can see how your little one has developed.

Have a guest book

You could place a special guest book on the top table. Think about having separate books if the ceremony is for more than one child. Write a foreword for the book, maybe echoing your hopes for your child's future, and ask friends and family to add their own personal messages.

Music

Generally speaking it's not a good idea to have music playing during the ceremony. However, if you have a talented guest who'd like to play a

musical tribute to your child – either something they've written specially or something else particularly appropriate – you might like to include it at the end of the ceremony.

Lighting a candle

A simple and very popular symbolic act is to light a special Naming Day candle. Displayed on the top table it could be lit at the very beginning of the ceremony, or perhaps during the actual naming, or to mark the closing of the ceremony. It's important the candle remains alight, so if you have the ceremony outside it's best to place it inside a vase or other glass vessel.

Top Tip!

If your ceremony is for more than one child, particularly twins, it's a good idea to develop a theme for each child. The easiest way to do this is with different colours to give each child a separate 'identity'.

The toast

This, of course, is one of the most popular ways to close a ceremony. As with everything, it's essential to plan the toast to ensure it goes smoothly.

If you're holding the ceremony at a venue and their staff will be serving drinks for the toast, give them an idea of when it'll be needed and agree a signal to indicate when they should pop the corks. Equally important is to determine the content of the toast in advance. It could be preceded by a short speech by one of the Supporting Adults, for example, or simply proposed by the Celebrant, a parent or a grandparent:

> " Would you all please raise your glasses in a toast… To Matthew – we wish you health, happiness and long life. "

To which your guests will naturally respond by repeating the salutation.

Make sure whoever is serving the drinks knows not to pop corks during the ceremony.

The best time to uncork the bottles is when certificates are being signed at the end. Make sure you've got a non-alcoholic bucks-fizz for the drivers and non-drinkers. Decide in advance who will act as toastmaster to avoid any last-minute confusion.

A special cake

Many married couples save the top layer of their wedding cake for an occasion like this. If this doesn't apply you could, of course, have a special cake made by one of your guests or a local bakery. An alternative would be a celebration cake from a supermarket, which you can ice or add a personalised Naming Day cake ribbon, available online. There are also some novel alternatives to a traditional cake. You could have a selection of homemade fairy cakes or cup cakes, each iced with the baby's name.

On a similar theme you could involve other children in making cookies or gingerbread men, again iced with the baby's name. Another fun alternative is a chocolate fountain.

A time capsule

Creating a time capsule is another great symbolic act, and is also one that involves all your guests. Just ask each of them to bring something personal for inclusion in the time capsule and 'bury' it at the end of the ceremony, or later on if you don't have the ceremony at home.

There are time capsules available that you can bury in the garden, but they're expensive because they're specially made to protect the contents. Most are only suitable for 'burying' in the loft, or in a garden shed, and cost around £20.

Releasing helium balloons

A fun way to close the ceremony, and one that involves all your guests, is to release helium balloons. You can pre-print tags with a message asking the finder to call you to let you know how far it travelled, and ask guests to add

There are all sorts of things you can include in your capsule . . .

- That day's newspaper

- A copy of the naming certificate

- A copy of the script

- Selection of Naming Day greeting cards

- That day's Top Twenty music chart

- A photo of the event

- Photos of guests with messages on the back

- A CD ROM of photos and news items

- A recorded message

- Keepsakes from the birth

- First Day Cover (stamps)

- New minted coins

- A homemade voucher promising a trip or a gift, to be redeemed on the child's 18th birthday

their name and a special message. You could even offer a prize for whoever's balloon goes furthest.

If you do plan a balloon race have a look at the Balloon Association's website www.nabas.co.uk as there are some regulations that may apply, especially if you release a large number of balloons.

Planting a tree

A longer-lasting dedication is to plant a tree or shrub in your child's honour. You can tag a sapling with a special message and you could even tie a ribbon round it every year to use it as a unique growth chart.

Dwarf trees are ideal for smaller gardens and patios, and don't grow taller than two metres. This can be ideal since it can be easily relocated if you move home.

Gift ideas

If you want to give your child a special gift to commemorate the day you'll probably want to make it something special and long-lasting. Since you'll receive gifts from many of your guests, and will probably have collected many mementos already, one good idea is a keepsake box. This could be something you have specially made and engraved, or it could simply be one that you've bought from a gift shop or online.

Ideas and themes

As for your guests, if the ceremony is being held just months after the birth of your child it's likely that many of them will have sent or given gifts fairly recently. If this is the case you might not want them to feel obliged to do so again. Perhaps you'd prefer to encourage your guests to bring, or provide, something more personal instead. Here are some ideas that you might find useful:

Just so you know . . . A range of high quality Thank You cards and gift ideas are available from www.civilceremonies.co.uk

'Traditional' gifts

- Money box

- Music box

- Gift basket of bibs, booties, etc

- Photo frame

- Napkin ring

- Silver spoon

- Candle

- Teddy bear

- Jewellery

- Something engraved with the child's name

- Something containing the child's birth-stone

Homemade gifts

If you'd prefer that guests not buy a gift, you could suggest either something handmade or symbolic. Some of your guests will have a hobby or a special skill that they could use to create a more personal gift. Handmade gifts are especially personal and meaningful, and will always be treasured.

Homemade gifts

- Poetry or prose

- Personalised story book

- Something embroidered

- A cushion or a quilt

- A painting or drawing

- A scrapbook

- A collage of photographs

- Hand-blown glass or something ceramic

- A wood or metal plaque

Symbolic gifts

- Donation to a charity that's close to your heart

- Sponsor a child in a third-world country

- Sponsor an endangered animal

- Dedicate a tree via the Woodland Trust

- Pledge to teach the child a special skill

Gifts to give to your guests

Many people like to present their guests with a special memento of the day. This could be something you present on the day, or something you put together and send on after the event, perhaps with a thank-you card.

Ideas for little gifts on the day include decorated eggs, either chocolate or made of wood. These symbolise birth and a new beginning. After the event you could send a framed photograph, either of the child or of the gathering. This could be a specially framed photo for the Supporting Adults and simple card-framed photos for everyone else.

If you plan to send thank-you cards make sure you make a note of the gift each guest brings so you can mention it when you write.

Easy
budgeting

As we've seen, a Naming Ceremony can be anything from an intimate family occasion to a large-scale event that includes a whole range of activities. How you plan your ceremony, where you hold it and what you include, will undoubtedly be influenced by the budget you decide to allocate to it.

ITEM	NOTES	COST
Ceremony Script		
Celebrant		
Venue		
Decoration		
Catering (Food)		
Catering (Drink)		
A Special Cake		
Photography		
New clothes		
Stationery		
Order of Ceremony		
Certificates		
Gifts		
Symbolic extras eg. Candles		
Entertainment		
GRAND TOTAL £		

Plan . . .
Use this budget guide to give you an overview of the likely costs, although some things (like venues) are obviously variable.

Your ceremony script

There are three types of script you can use in your ceremony . . .

1. A script you write yourself from scratch using this book as a guide.

Everything you need to create the structure of your ceremony is contained within the pages of this book. There are also examples of the kind of promises you might want to make to help you formulate your own, and samples of popular readings. Aside from the time it will take you to create it there's obviously no cost involved. However, you might feel it's a bit of an onerous task and that you'd rather have the script professionally prepared for you.

2. A professionally written script that's based on a template.

This is a relatively inexpensive script that's written for you by a professional ceremony provider. You're provided with a pack that includes a structured template and selections of appropriate wording for every part of the script, including Parents' Promises, Supporting Adults' Promises and various readings. You simply personalise the template and make your choices from the selections of wording provided, and the script is then created according to those choices. A script like this is likely to cost between £50 and £70.

3. A professionally written 'bespoke' script.

This is a more comprehensive scripting option that will give you an essential structure, but without the restrictions of a rigid template. It'll give you much more freedom of expression by letting you expand the structure and include your own wording in addition to selecting from a large range of suggested words and phrases. Some companies will have a dedicated 'bespoke' script team who work with you to make the script totally unique and personal. A script like this is likely to cost between £100 and £130.

A professional Celebrant

Although you can have your ceremony led by someone you know, it's not hard to see why most families choose to have a professional Celebrant conduct their ceremony.

A professional Celebrant understands what you want to achieve and is dedicated to helping you enjoy the perfect ceremony. He or she will be expert at putting guests at ease, creating the right atmosphere and tone, and will guide you seamlessly through every stage of the ceremony.

It's important to choose a Celebrant who's professionally trained, who works to a strict code of practice and who has the support of a dedicated ceremony creation team. This will give you absolute confidence in both their ability and the integrity of the service they'll provide you with.

As part of their service, the Celebrant should meet you before the date of the ceremony. This gives you both an opportunity to get to know each other and gives you the peace of mind that he or she will conduct the ceremony exactly as you wish. It's also an opportunity to discuss the ceremony itself in detail so you both know what to expect.

A professional Celebrant will cost from around £100 to about £160 depending on the complexity of the ceremony and the extent of the service they'll provide on the day.

The Venue

The venue is likely to be one of your largest costs if you decide not to hold the ceremony at home. Prices for hotels and community venues vary widely depending on where you live. Remember that a venue doesn't have to be licensed to host a Naming Ceremony.

Decorating the venue

You can use all manner of items to decorate the venue, such as balloons and banners, either homemade or bought specially for the occasion. They could be in whatever your colour theme is and can be personalised with your child's name. These are guide prices for some of the most popular items available online.

You can also buy simple flower arrangements very reasonably from your local florist or supermarket. Or perhaps one of your guests has an abundant garden and can provide an arrangement for you.

- Naming Day Balloons (pink or blue): from £4.50 for 10

- Naming Day Personalised Banners: from £1.50 per metre

- Naming Day Personalised Ribbon: from £1.20 per metre

- Personalised Naming Day Candles (pink or blue): from £7.50

Top Tip!
Including some homemade decorations adds a very special and personal touch. It's also a great way to involve the family!

Easy budgeting

Providing food for your guests

What you spend on food depends on where the ceremony's being held and the time of day.

At a hotel or similar venue, a light lunch or high tea could cost as little as £6 or as much as £15 or more per head. It all depends on the quality and location of the venue. An evening buffet is likely to cost between £10 to £20 per head.

Don't forget to consider the number of children in your party, for whom the price per head should be lower.

For a ceremony at home or at a venue where you're providing your own catering you obviously have much greater control over the costs. It shouldn't cost more than a few pounds per head for even a quite sumptuous buffet or picnic spread.

Providing drinks

How you budget for drinks is entirely up to you. Although guests will generally expect to be fed, few will expect you to cover a bar bill too. Bear in mind that if you're having the ceremony at home, unlike for a normal party most guests won't think to bring a bottle unless they're specifically asked.

Some hotels, especially smaller, privately owned hotels, will be happy to agree a special deal for providing a quantity of specific 'house' wines, but you're unlikely to be able to negotiate on anything else. You could provide a certain amount of wine and soft drinks with the meal and let guests pay for further drinks at the bar.

As a guide to providing a reasonable selection of drinks at home, you might consider the following a fair assumption. Bear in mind that many of your guests will be driving, whereas others may get very much in the party mood and consume the drivers' share!

- Half a bottle of wine per guest: £2.50 per head

- Two or three cans or bottles of beer per guest: £2 per head

- A bottle of gin and a bottle of vodka: £20 total

- Half a dozen litre bottles of tonic water: £3 total

- Plenty of fruit juice, cola, lemonade, etc: £15 total

Having a toast . . .?
(Allow one bottle per five or six guests)

- A reasonable quality Champagne: £3.50 per head, Or . . .

- Cava or a sparkling Chardonnay: £1 per head

- Non-alcoholic Bucks-fizz: 50p per head

Remember . . .
Don't forget to buy plenty of ice and a few lemons or limes.

A special cake

If you don't know someone who can bake a special cake for you, you could either have one made by a local bakery for around £30 or buy a celebration cake from a supermarket for about £10 and simply ice it to make it personal.

Photography

You can arrange a professional photographer if your budget permits. Expect to spend a good two or three hundred pounds hiring one. However, you're likely to have at least a few guests who possess a good quality digital camera, and are proficient using it.

Aside from providing you with a good selection of photos, or a DVD of the event, some of your guests are bound to be computer-savvy enough to create an online photo album for everyone to view after the event.

Stationery

It's nice to personalise the event as much as possible, and to make it extra special by using proper invitations and other stationery. Of course, that doesn't necessarily mean buying everything. It can be a lot of fun creating your own, or involving older children in making them.

Some items, like certificates, need to look professional to mirror the importance of the event and are relatively inexpensive to buy.

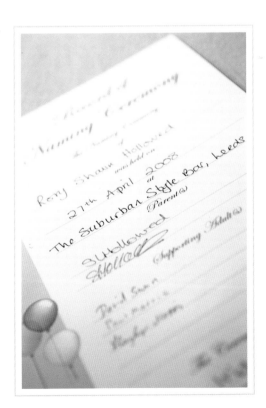

- Naming day invitations: from about £3 upwards for 10

- A special Naming Ceremony guest book: around £20 to £25

- Order of Ceremony: provided free*

- Naming certificate (parents): provided free*

- Naming certificate (Supporting Adults): about £3.50

- Naming certificate (grandparents): about £3.50

- Naming day napkins: about £4 to £5 for 15

- Naming Ceremony thank-you cards: about £4 to £5 for 10

*Just so you know
A professional ceremony company should provide the original Order of Ceremony free of charge. You can photocopy it for your guests if you wish. A certificate for the parents should also be included.

Gifts

It's impossible to say how much you should spend on a special Naming Day gift for your child. It depends totally on what you consider appropriate, and it isn't necessary to buy anything. You might decide to have something specially made by hand, such as a wooden keepsake box or treasure chest. Alternatively you could consider a special naming day money box, teddy bear or keepsake box from a specialist naming gift online shop.

If you want to give something to your Supporting Adults a quality framed photograph is a nice idea. Likewise for grandparents. For your other guests, eggs made of chocolate or wood (which represent birth and a new beginning) make an appropriate little gift and are available from many good gift shops.

If you like the idea of releasing helium balloons you could either buy multiple packs of Naming Day balloons for around £4 to £5 per 10, or simply buy a bulk pack of ordinary balloons (but make

Whatever entertainment you decide to provide it's wise to get three quotes to ensure you get the best deal.

New clothes

Unlike a wedding it's not necessary to buy a new outfit unless you want to. The only likely expense is if you want to buy something special for your child to wear for the ceremony.

sure they're suitable for being filled with helium). The gas itself can be purchased from a local supplier or online. A helium cylinder to inflate 50 balloons will cost about £30 or so.

If you're struck by the idea of planting a tree, you can buy a suitable sapling or older tree from any good garden centre. A dwarf tree is a good idea for a small garden, and should cost little more than £30 or so.

Entertainment

If you're planning to make the most of a garden party, or extend the celebrations into the evening at a hotel, there are many things you can do to provide your guests with entertainment. For example, you could hire a bouncy castle, a children's entertainer, or a disco.

Authors note

I truly hope this book has given you a real picture of what Naming Ceremonies are and how you can arrange one. Furthermore, I hope it has inspired in you a desire to create a very personal Naming Ceremony for your child that includes and reflects whatever you want it to. These ceremonies are flexible for today's families – for your family circumstances, whatever they may be. As Bel Mooney says in her foreword, what matters most is simply your desire to promise, in front of your family and friends, who witness, to be as good a parent as you can be.

It doesn't matter whether you are having a Celebrant to conduct the ceremony or if you are conducting it yourself or asking someone you know to lead it for you. Neither does it matter whether you are holding it in a stately home or your own garden. What's important is that at the core of this very personal and meaningful ceremony will be the love that you have for your child.

Whatever type of ceremony you decide to have, I hope you have a truly wonderful day that provides you with memories that will last a lifetime.

Warmest wishes,

Anne Barber

PS - Many families very kindly write to me about their experiences and some of their comments are included here. I would also like to open that invitation to you. Whether you organise the ceremony yourself or ask us to organise it for you, I would love to hear about your special day and how this book has helped you. My address details are on the 'Useful Contacts' page.

A lovely way of showing everyone how loved and important our daughter is to us

It was brilliant, actually better than I expected it to be

The Ceremony was very important to us, you are welcoming your child to the world and you want things to be perfect

The day made me feel very bonded to my baby and her dad, which was really important especially after bad post natal depression

Lots of sensible advice from the Celebrant, such as not getting our baby too excited beforehand

A great opportunity to establish our son as a member of the extended family

The Celebrant was great and personalised the ceremony for us – even when our son blew raspberries!

Our guests thought the ceremony was well presented and meaningful for our child

The ceremony day was the highlight of his first year. Nothing compared during the year with this

Everyone felt very involved in the ceremony

The order of the ceremony flowed really well

The poems and readings were really touching I could not have hoped for anything better

An essential checklist

Here's a simple checklist to help you ensure nothing gets forgotten when planning your ceremony. Not everything will apply but it will help you to keep track of what needs to be organised.

ITEM	SUPPLIERS / NOTES	TICK or ENTER
Guest List		Total adults: Total children:
Venue		Confirmed venue: Confirmed numbers: Confirmed menu:
Celebrant		Confirmed:
Invitations		Written: Posted:
Supporting Adults		Promises agreed: Promises agreed: Promises agreed:
Other Participants		Contribution agreed: Contribution agreed: Contribution agreed:
Ceremony Script		Started: Completed:
Readings		Reader: Reader: Reader:

Food		Hot: Cold: Vegetarian:
Drink		Alcohol: Soft drinks: The Toast:
Cake		
Entertainment		Confirmed: Confirmed:
Symbolic Acts		Confirmed: Confirmed:
Photography		Photography: Video:
Decorations		
Certificates		Supporting Adults: Grandparents:
Other Stationery		Order of Ceremony: Guest Book: Thank You Cards:
Special Clothes		For You: For Your Child:
Gifts		For Your Child Supporting Adults: For Other Guests:

Useful contacts

Civil Ceremonies Ltd
www.civilceremonies.co.uk

A professional ceremony provider with national coverage. Provides complete ceremony packages with a Celebrant, and also script-only options. Also supplies Naming Ceremony stationery, accessories and gifts, and plans to include a national database of venues and suppliers.

Bounty
www.bounty.com

The UK's premier parenting club packed with helpful information and advice for you and your baby. Also features baby product reviews and online forums.

The Parents Centre
www.parentscentre.gov.uk

Government website devoted to parenting that includes a huge range of useful information.

Meet a Mum Association
www.mama.co.uk

A useful website that provides online forums for mums to exchange information on a wide range of issues relating to parenting.

The Poetry Archive
www.poetryarchive.org

A website that includes a large database of poetry, including poems for children.

The Woodland Trust
www.woodlandtrust.org.uk

An organisation devoted to woodland preservation that includes a scheme to dedicate a tree and provides information about planting a tree.

The Balloon Association
www.nabas.co.uk

Provides essential information for anyone planning a balloon release during their ceremony.

The 100 Year Website
www.the100yearwebsite.com

A website that provides an online 'time capsule' service.

Time Tin
www.timetin.com

A website that provides time capsules for 'burial' at home.

Marquee Hire Directory
www.performancetextiles.org.uk

Includes an online directory of marquee hirers that you can search by area.

Children's Entertainers
www.equity.org.uk

Includes an online directory of children's entertainers who are members of this organisation.

General Register Office
www.gro.gov.uk

Information about registering a birth or changing a child's name.

Making a Will
www.adviceguide.org.uk

Website of the Citizens Advice Bureau that includes information about making a will.

Finding a Will-Writer
www.willwriters.com

Includes an online database that you can search by area.

The Young Foundation
www.youngfoundation.org.uk

Website devoted to furthering the work of Lord Young, who created the Baby Naming Society.

NSPCC
www.nspcc.org.uk

The national charity that's dedicated to protecting children from cruelty.

Save the Children
www.savethechildren.org.uk

The national charity that campaigns to save the lives of children around the world.

The Children's Society
www.childrenssociety.org.uk

The national charity that provides help and understanding for children who are unable to find the support they need elsewhere.

Gingerbread
www.oneparentfamilies.org.uk

Gingerbread is an organisation for Lone Parent Families. In May 2007 it merged with The National Council for One Parent Families.

About Civil Ceremonies Ltd

Civil Ceremonies Ltd has been instrumental to the introduction, availability and enormous growth in the popularity of Naming Ceremonies since the concept was first proposed by a government white-paper in 1998.

Integral to this government proposal was the pioneering work of the labour peer, Lord Young of Dartington. Lord Young, who died in 2002, was renowned as one of the world's most creative social thinkers and doers. In the wake of a continual decline of baptisms since the 1940s, and in recognition of a widely perceived deterioration of family values, Lord Young created the Baby Naming Society in 1994. The Society was formed to promote baby welcoming ceremonies and joint parental responsibility.

A pilot-scheme for registrars to offer the new naming ceremonies to families was launched in 1999. The scheme was set up by Anne Barber, who later founded Civil Ceremonies Ltd, and was developed in partnership with the Baby Naming Society. Families welcomed this new choice of civil ceremony and the pilot-scheme proved extremely successful. The scheme was subsequently rolled out nationally.

The formation of Civil Ceremonies Ltd in 2002 by Anne Barber, who is the company's Managing Director, created a company whose aim was to develop Naming Ceremonies to a professional level and promote their accessibility to families throughout the UK. Civil Ceremonies Ltd now incorporates the Baby Naming Society, and its former Director, Rosie Styles, co-ordinates the scripting of 'bespoke' ceremonies for the company.

Civil Ceremonies Ltd is the only company offering a nationwide service and is proud of its excellent reputation. The company is ISO9001 accredited and is dedicated to providing professional and affordable ceremonies of the highest quality. Civil Ceremonies

Ltd continues to offer ceremonies through the registration service, but additionally operates its own stringent training and development programme. The company now has several hundred professionally trained Celebrants throughout the country performing thousands of ceremonies every year.

In addition to the ceremonies performed by its Celebrants, the company now also provides a 'script only' service for families who prefer not to have a professional Celebrant. Other developments have seen the introduction of a 'bespoke' option, which give families greater choice for the content and structure of their ceremony, and special birthday and Christmas ceremonies.

The growth in popularity of Naming Ceremonies led to a strong demand for other types of ceremony. This resulted in the creation of a ceremony to celebrate a Renewal of Marriage Vows, and to the development of other personal ceremonies for married and non-married couples. The company now also offers Wedding Celebration Ceremonies, Partnership Ceremonies and Commitment Ceremonies.

Under the steerage of Anne Barber, Civil Ceremonies Ltd retains its strong sense of moral obligation to the spirit of Lord Young's vision. As the 21st Century progresses, Civil Ceremonies Ltd remains committed to its founding principals and is dedicated to helping families celebrate special events in their lives with highly professional and affordable personal ceremonies.

CivilCeremoniesLtd
worth remembering

Acknowledgements

Thanks go to Rosie Styles whose extensive knowledge of these ceremonies and special ceremony wording has been drawn upon throughout. To David Hayles whose wonderful copywriting skills have worked their magic and to Krysia Niezgoda for unfailing support and marketing expertise. Special thanks to our amazing designer and consultant, Gemma Barber, whose hard work and insight into these ceremonies has made this book look exactly the way we wanted it to. Her expertise and advice has been invaluable. Thank you Gemma.

Grateful thanks to the following wonderful families who so kindly let us photograph their ceremonies and talked to us so enthusiastically about what their day meant to them. Stacey, Shaun & Rory Hollowed; Angela, David, Freja, Alicia & Willow Jasper; Laura, John, Sam & Scarlett Clough; Jo, John & Eleanor Musto; Jessica Kirby, Glen & Isla Borrell; David, Nicola & Amber Jaques.

Finally a huge thank you to the Celebrants across the UK and the administrative team led by Marilyn Watts, all of whom give so much of themselves to make the ceremonies special.

Photo credits
Cooper Photography 8, 20-21, 23, 28-29, 31, 32, 35, 38, 46t, 50-51, 53, 54, 63, 65, 66, 70, 82, 83, 85, 91, 92, 95, 99, 104, 108, 111b, 120, 125, 128; Faye Hatton Photography 14-15, 22, 24, 27, 45, 56-57, 64, 93, 106, 109; Key Reflections 10, 12, 16, 33, 36-37, 61, 62, 80; Cinnamon Photography 42-43, 44, 46b, 55, 71, 76-77, 79, 81, 88-89, 90, 98, 110, 111t; Robin-Allison-Smith 9; Chris Alvanas 11; Richard Sweet 3; Fazakas Tibor 72; Steve Woods 100-101.

Every effort has been made to contact copyright holders, but should there be any errors or omissions we would be pleased to insert the appropriate acknowledgement in any subsequent printing of this publication.

Index

Index

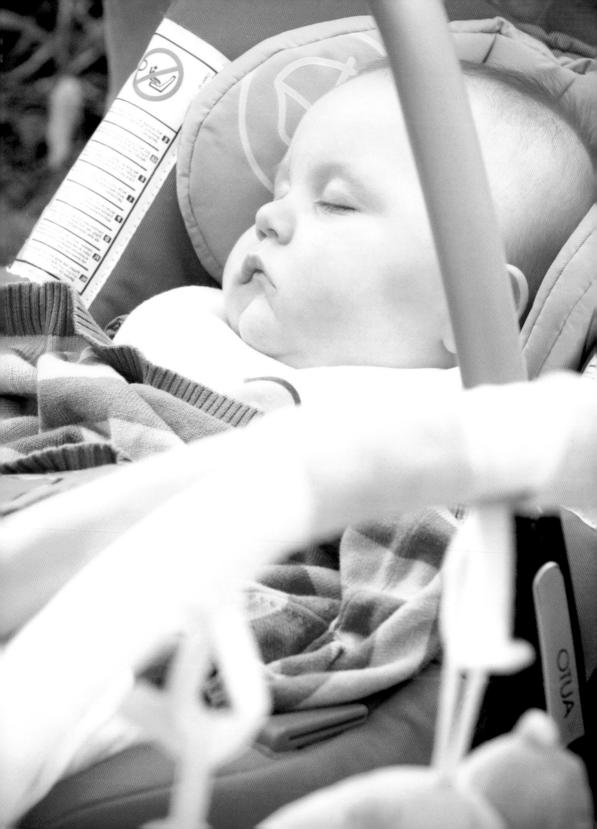

My notes . . .

My notes . . .